IDENTIFICATION OF PERSONALITY CHARACTERISTICS AND SELF-CONCEPT FACTORS OF BATTERED WIVES

By Lorraine M. Hartik

PALO ALTO, CALIFORNIA

Published By

R & E RESEARCH ASSOCIATES
936 Industrial Avenue
Palo Alto, California 94303

Library of Congress Card Catalog Number
81-83620

I. S. B. N.
0-88247-618-1

Copyright 1982
By

Lorraine M. Hartik

ACKNOWLEDGEMENTS

To the memory of Dr. Sidney Jourard, whose initial encouragement has kept me working,

To Dr. Sherry Skidmore, whose continuing presence, guidance, encouragement and invaluable friendship throughout the many phases of graduate school and this study have helped me reach this point,

To Betty Ruth Goode, whose long-term acquaintance and support made pursuit of this study possible,

To Dr. Sam Krug, whose technical advice and enthusiasm kept me accurate and precise and determined, and

Most of all, to my subjects who shall remain nameless, for their courage and trust in sharing themselves so that others might benefit from their openness, I dedicate this effort.

TABLE OF CONTENTS

	Page
LIST OF TABLES	ix
LIST OF FIGURES	xi

Chapter

1. INTRODUCTION 1
    - PROBLEM STATEMENT 2
    - SIGNIFICANCE OF THE STUDY 2
    - PURPOSE OF THE STUDY 3
    - RESEARCH HYPOTHESES 3
    - DEFINITION OF TERMS 4
        - Battered Wife 4
        - Husband 4
        - Personality Characteristics . . 4
        - Personality Profile 6
        - Self-concept 6
    - DELIMITATIONS OF THE STUDY 8
    - ASSUMPTIONS 9
    - SUMMARY 9

Chapter		Page
2.	REVIEW OF SELECTED LITERATURE . . .	11
	BRITISH LITERATURE	13
	AMERICAN LITERATURE	17
	SUMMARY	24
3.	DESIGN AND PROCEDURE	26
	NULL HYPOTHESES	26
	SUBJECTS	27
	INSTRUMENTATION	28
	Sixteen Personality Factor Questionnaire (16PF) Form A .	29
	Tennessee Self Concept Scale (TSCS)	31
	PROCEDURE	33
	DATA ANALYSIS	34
4.	RESULTS	35
	HYPOTHESIS 1--NULL FORM	36
	HYPOTHESIS 2--NULL FORM	38
	HYPOTHESIS 3--NULL FORM	38
	HYPOTHESIS 4--NULL FORM	41
	ADDITIONAL RESULTS	41
	SUMMARY	44
5.	DISCUSSION, CONCLUSIONS AND RECOMMENDATIONS	48
	DISCUSSION	48
	CONCLUSIONS	49

Chapter		Page
5. RECOMMENDATIONS		54
SUMMARY		55
METHOD		57
Hypothesis 1		57
Hypothesis 2		57
Hypothesis 3		57
Hypothesis 4		57
RESULTS		58
ADDITIONAL RESULTS		59
BIBLIOGRAPHY		60
APPENDIXES		
A. DESCRIPTIONS OF SUBJECTS		72
B. SUMMARY OF MEANS AND STANDARD DEVIATIONS FOR THE 16PF AND TSCS SCORES		80
C. THE QUESTIONNAIRES		83

LIST OF TABLES

Table		Page
1.	Sixteen Personality Factor Questionnaire - Form A	30
2.	Tennessee Self Concept Scale . . .	32
3.	Summary of Analysis of Variance of Personality Characteristics Battered and Non-Battered Wives	37
4.	Summary of Analysis of Variance of Self-Concept Factors of Battered and Non-Battered Wives	40
5.	Summary of Analysis of Variance of Second Order and Derivative Characteristics of the 16PF for Battered and Non-Battered Wives	43
6.	Summary of Analysis of Variance of Additional Factors of the TSCS for Battered and Non-Battered Wives	45

LIST OF FIGURES

Figure		Page
1.	Summary Personality Profile of Battered and Non-Battered Wives	39
2.	TSCS Summary Profile Sheet of Battered and Non-Battered Wives	42

CHAPTER 1

INTRODUCTION

Wife battering has been a means of keeping women subordinated to men in patriarchal societies since their inception in pre-Biblical times (Martin, 1976). It is a complex problem, encompassing historical attitudes toward women, the institution of marriage, the economy, the intricacies of criminal and civil law, and the delivery system of social service agencies. The American public and the government has only begun to take notice since 1974 of this problem, following the lead of Great Britain, who, in 1971, established a refuge for battered women in London known as Chiswick (Gibbens, 1975).

Studies of wife beating as a sociological phenomenon in the United States has been undertaken in explorations of violence within families, and in relation to child abuse (Steinmetz and Straus, 1974) as a result of pioneer work in England (Scott, 1974; Daly, 1975; Gayford, 1975).

Many myths exist about the battered woman, as evidenced by Mildred Pagelow in a paper presented at the Second International Symposium on Victimology (Boston, Massachusetts, 1976). What the battered wife is like, and how she views herself is still presently unclear (Nichols, 1975).

PROBLEM STATEMENT

The personality sphere concept, a design that insures coverage for all behavior that commonly is described to make up personality as a whole, is the central feature of questionnaires by Cattell (1973). Fitts (1965) conceived that the individual's concept of himself has been highly influential in much of his behavior and is also directly related to his general personality. The study addresses the personality characteristics and self-concept factors of wives who have been battered. The problem of the study might be further clarified by asking two questions.

1. Do personality characteristics differ in wives who have been battered from those of wives who have not been battered?

2. Does the self-concept differ in battered wives from that of non-battered wives?

SIGNIFICANCE OF THE STUDY

The problem examined in the study is important for several reasons. First, the study will add to the sparse literature and research on personality characteristics of battered wives. Second, a personality profile may be developed of the battered wife. Third, the study will contribute to the literature and research on the self-concept of battered wives. Finally, the study may provide some insights into the psychological makeup of battered wives which could be useful by professional workers in developing treatment plans.

PURPOSE OF THE STUDY

In the research of Cattell (1970), indication of a generalized profile of the personality has been created, and distinction has been made among diagnostic groups of various types. At the present time, no specific personality profile for battered wives has been established by testing. As mentioned, many myths of what the battered wife is like continue to exist. Fitts (1965), like Cattell, has developed differentiation in self-concept profiles between several pathological groups, but very few profiles exist for specific social groups such as the battered wife. The purpose of the research, then, is to identify personality characteristics and self-concept factors of battered wives and develop profiles, as measured by selected psychological instruments.

RESEARCH HYPOTHESES

1. Wives who have been battered will evidence different personality characteristics from non-battered wives as measured by the Sixteen Personality Factor Questionnaire.

2. Wives who have been battered will evidence a different personality profile from non-battered wives as measured by the Sixteen Personality Factor Questionnaire.

3. There is a significant difference between the self-concept factors of battered wives and non-battered wives as measured by the Tennessee Self Concept Scale.

4. Wives who have been battered will evidence a different self-concept profile from

non-battered wives as measured by the Tennessee Self Concept Scale.

DEFINITION OF TERMS

The following terms are provided to facilitate the understanding of terms as utilized in the study:

Battered Wife. A woman who has been physically beaten on more than one occasion by her mate, with severity enough to require medical attention, or which can be witnessed upon her person.

Husband. The man who inflicted the battering on his wife.

Personality Characteristics. For the study, those sixteen trait dimensions described by Raymond Cattell (1970):

Factor A, Reserved-Outgoing: at the low level, an inclination to be cautious in emotional expression, and at the high level, a tendency to express a full spectrum of effect.

Factor B, Less Intelligent-More Intelligent: shows low mental capacity and higher mental capacity.

Factor C, Affected by Feelings-Emotionally Stable: dynamic integration and maturity as opposed to uncontrolled, disorganized emotionality. Considered a measure of ego strength.

Factor E, Humble-Assertive: submissiveness versus dominance.

Factor F, Sober-Happy-go-lucky: primary component in extraversion. Low reflects introspective behavior, and high indicates extraversion tendencies.

Factor G, Expedient-Conscientious: commonly considered a measure of super-ego strength or conscience.

Factor H, Shy-Venturesome: indicates appreciable constitutional and autonomic temperament indicators, and tends to reflect the activity as shown attitude-behaviorally of the autonomic nervous system.

Factor I, Toughminded-Tenderminded: indicates at low scores the tendency to be self-reliant and "hard", while high scores evidence an expectation of attention and help-seeking behavior.

Factor L, Trusting-Suspicious: a trait involved in the process of interpersonal relationships. A low score generally indicates a personality easy to get along with, while a high score may show itself in the form of disruptive behavior in interpersonal relationships.

Factor M, Practical-Imaginative: shows the tendency toward practical reality orientation at the low end, and the tendency to be fanciful and absorbed in ideas at the high end of the continuum.

Factor N, Forthright-Shrewd: at a low score level, the tendency to be unpretentious, showing a blind faith in human nature, and at the high score level, the tendency to be socially aware, and insightful regarding both self and others.

Factor O, Self-Assured-Apprehensive: indicates untroubled adequacy versus self-reproaching and guilt-prone tendencies.

Factor Q_1, Conservative-Experimenting: the dimension reflecting tolerance for traditional, established ideas at a low score level, and the tendency to analyze, experiment and try new ways at a high score level.

Factor Q_2, Group Dependent-Self Sufficient: is the tendency to be a joiner or sound follower at a low score level, and resourceful, preferring one's own decisions at a high score level.

Factor Q_3, Undisciplined Self Conflict-Control: indicates whether behavior tends toward carelessness of protocol or social preciseness.

Factor Q_4, Relaxed-Tense: shows low ergic tension at a low score position and high tension and frustration at the upper end of the continuum. High is best interpreted as an "id" energy excited in excess of the ego strength capacity to discharge it, and is generally disruptive of steady application and emotional balance.

Personality Profile. The overall pattern on a sten continuum format, presented by scores of the subject of the sixteen personality factors described above.

Self-concept. How the individual perceives herself. Fitts (1965) differentiates sixteen factors in the Tennessee Self Concept Scale, to be used in the study, as follows:

1. Total self concept: a measure of the individual overall self-esteem.

1.1 Identity, which answers "who am I?"

1.2 Self-satisfaction, concerned with how well the individual accepts who she is.

1.3 Behavior, concerned with how a person perceives how she acts.

1.4 Physical, concerned with how a person sees herself in relation to her body, health, physical appearance, skills and her sexuality.

1.5 Moral-ethical self, concerned with how the person sees herself in relation to her moral worth, feelings about God, perception of what kind of a person she is and how satisfied she is with her religion or lack of it.

1.6 Personal self, concerned with the person's perception of her personal worth, feelings of adequacy and an evaluation of personality apart from her body.

1.7 Family self, concerned with how the person perceives her worth, value and adequacy as a family member.

1.8 Social self, concerned with how the person perceives herself in relation to others, how the person reflects a sense of adequacy and worth in social interactions.

1.9 Self criticism, concerned with truthfulness of response, distortion and defensiveness.

2. Defensive positive, is concerned with more refined measures of defensiveness.

3. General maladjustment, concerned with the person's general mental health--adjustment or maladjustment.

4. Psychosis, concerned with person's basic personality weakness and defects, in particular, the degree of psychotic reactions.

5. Personality disorder, concerned with the person's basic personality defects and weaknesses.

6. Neurosis, concerned with the degree of similarity or dissimilarity of the person with neurotic patients.

7. Personality integration, concerned with differentiating those individuals who are high in their personality integration from other groups.

<u>Self Concept Profile</u>. The overall pattern on a T-score and mean format of scores of subjects of the self-concept factors above.

DELIMITATIONS OF THE STUDY

For the purposes of the study, the following delimitations are apparent:

1. The study was restricted geographically to San Bernardino County of California, U.S.A. Care should be exercised in extrapolating the results to other geographic areas.

2. The population sample was limited to women who had been battered by their husbands, and women who had never been battered.

3. Subjects were limited to those who completed the questionnaires on a voluntary basis.

4. Subjects were limited to those who could read at or above the sixth grade level, and were not institutionally confined.

ASSUMPTIONS

1. It was assumed that the Sixteen Personality Factor Questionnaire (16PF) is a valid and reliable instrument for measuring personality characteristics (Cattell, Eber and Tatsuoka, 1972).

2. It was assumed that the Tennessee Self Concept Scale (TSCS) is a valid and reliable instrument for measuring and differentiating aspects of the self-concept (Fitts, 1973).

3. It was assumed that the self-reporting by wives that they had been battered was truthfully reported, and no attempt to check medical or legal records was made.

SUMMARY

Both the public and social agencies in America are becoming more aware of the need for changes in laws, attitudes, and practices in dealing with wife-battering. Originally surfacing as a social and family problem in Great Britain, within the last decade attention in America has turned to violence in the family, first in relation to child-beating, and now, to the battered wife problem. Literature indicates a paucity of research on the battered wife herself or the batterer. It is assumed this lack is due in part to the recent focus upon the family and its social problems. The study aims at identification of the personality characteristics and self concept factors of the battered wife herself, through use of selected psychological instruments.

CHAPTER 2

REVIEW OF SELECTED LITERATURE

There is an enormous amount of literature available regarding the family and its various forms of interaction. There is an almost endless discussion of the many theories produced over the years, created to explain violence, with the focus shifting from the family group to the individual only within the past five years. The literature review is by necessity and design, limited to a historical perspective and brief overview of some major approaches within the past two decades to wife-battering both in England and the United States. Those pioneering writings have served to provide the present focus upon the wife-beating problem. Their perspective has been primarily either sociological or legal in focus, and lack the statistical empiricism of the psychological approach.

In one very real sense battered women are the only experts on their own situation. One drawback to research with battered women is the dificulty of deciding what the results mean and the use that will be made of them. Research is usually put forward as being "scientific" and "objective", free from prejudice, and based on facts, not opinion. Research never starts from a blank page, hence this is not always true.

Even what is known as empirical evidence can be interpreted according to the philosophy or point of view of the researcher. In discussing battered women as an unusual or abnormal event, assumptions are made about what is usual or normal in private family life. Not only have massive amounts been written by sociologists, psychologists, psychiatrists and journalists about family life, but most people belong to a family and have personal experience of relations' or friends' families. All that is individually felt that is known about family life is based on personal impression. Valuable as this experience may be, it provides no real idea how representative it is in society.

One purpose of research is in fact to measure, or try to measure the extent of various family patterns and ways of behaving in the family. Some things can be measured easier than others. Value judgments and standards of normality soon enter. It is harder still to define what certain forms of behavior mean in the context in which they occur. There has been, for example, a problem even about defining what a battered woman is. In practice, wife battering has come by general consent to mean physical assault of some degree of regularity, but this is a rough definition, and leads to another problem--that of defining what this violence means to those actually involved.

Existing research does in fact suggest that wife beating is not unusual. Before the subject began to be discussed publicly, no one collected statistics about it. More attempts to do so are being made today. Difficulties arise because people are not anxious to discuss wife battering, and are able to hide the facts in most cases. Various sources do provide some information, however. American divorce statistics show that physical abuse was given as a cause for divorce in one-third of all petitions. There are probably many more battered women than statistics will ever show, however, since many stay quietly within their situations. The existing shelters have found that many women who do leave feel too ashamed to talk about it, and the battering husband rarely will discuss it, even with friends (Lystad, 1975).

BRITISH LITERATURE

Erin Pizzey in London, in her book, <u>Scream Quietly or the Neighbours Will Hear</u> (1974), described how the first shelter for battered wives, Chiswick, came into being, and how it eventually sheltered thousands of battered wives and their children after they had sought help from the law, the National Health Service, or the social services of Great Britain, to no avail. As one of the founders and leaders of the movement to help battered women, she described, using mainly the words of the women and children themselves, the nature of the problem, the way in which the shelters that now exist in England came into being, and the battles that had to be fought with an indifferent world. She concluded her account with a plan of campaign for future action, now being used successfully, though slowly, in England. The book has had a definite impact--it has even been made into a television documentary--shown in America in the middle of the night!

Periodical literature in England dealt with wife-beating from within the context of the family grouping initially. Snell, Rosenwald, and Robey (1964), within the psychiatric clinic setting, described a family structure in which they found an essential ingredient for violence to be the need for both husband and wife for periodic reversal of roles--she to be punished, he to reestablish his masculine identity. Alcoholism was considered an important factor in the situation of role alteration. The study itself presented no empirical investigative evidence, and based its conclusions on review of cases treated at the clinic. Two case presentations were given which described in detail the situation and then provided an analysis of them. Mention was made in the article that thirty-seven men charged by their wives with assault and battery were referred to the clinic over a period of five years. It was from these that the conclusions of the study were drawn. It would appear that the very nature of the court-referral to the clinic provided an inhibiting factor to the results of the research. There was no indication that wives were involved in the study, though it was presented as a "study of family interaction."

P. D. Scott (1974) in an article on battered wives, discussed the similarities between wife battering and other forms of deviant behavior. Scott defined wife battering as a failure of adaptation. Classifying wife battering similarities in terms of the following, Scott saw the problem as largely a sociological phenomenon: a small "malignant" hard core which is difficult to influence. Scott discussed whether or not a relationship existed between wife battering and baby-battering, citing earlier research by Dr. Selwyn Smith, whose evidence was inconclusive. It is interesting that the study cited dealt with husbands who had been investigated legally for child-battering, while no mention was made of the possibility that battered wives may be battering mothers. Scott observed a sado-masochistic element in that a battering couple frequently returned to one another, though there was no discussion by contrast, of how many stayed apart. In Scott's study, the population was not clearly defined numerically, though mention was made of the fact that subjects were in Holloway Prison and Wandsworth Prison when originally examined in the research from which he drew his several conclusions. Scott felt that classification of wife battering was essential, and that most of the classifications of deviant behavior and criminality could be applied. He also stated that a great deal of descriptive research was a necessary part of obtaining this knowledge.

One of the best-known and most-quoted research studies done in England by Dr. Jasper Gayford (1975) proved to be statistically non-viable. Dr. Gayford used the interview method with nearly two hundred women who were staying at Chiswick Women's Aid in London. The replies he received were cut down to one hundred in reporting his research, with the other hundred discarded for no stated reason. Gayford therefore based his entire findings about battered women on the evidence from the one hundred women he selected, admitting that the women at Chiswick were "untypical" to begin with. They were a self-selected group, and not an average cross-section of the population. Gayford had no control group of non-battered women to compare them with. He seemed to feel it was significant that of his sample only sixty-five were brought up by both parents to the age of fifteen, and that eighty-five of the women had sexual intercourse without birth control before marriage or going to live with the man concerned. But one may ask, what does this really mean? Gayford attached an importance to the fact of sex without contraception which implied that he felt such behavior was uncommon in society at large. But was it? One must ask of his conclusions, how many couples like those described do not end up as battered women and wife-beating husbands?

A smaller study was done by Marsden and Owens (1975), in England, a study of nineteen women who had been battered but who had not gone to a refuge. Marsden came up with findings very different from Gayford's, using nonempirical methods. Marsden found little evidence for a "cycle of violence" being passed from generation to generation as Gayford had implied in his study. The women did not come from violent homes, and the men had no records of violence as in Gayford's study. On the other hand, Marsden did comment that most of the women in his study felt that their husbands showed an unreasonable wish to dominate them. They said they had been criticized for their untidiness, childishness, immaturity and irresponsibility. Such criticisms appeared to the wives to be partly due to old-fashioned and authoritarian attitudes, and changing attitudes among the women themselves as to what degree of equality there should be in marriage; Gayford never took any of this into account.

Returning to Gayford, he interviewed only wives, not husbands. His conclusions about men are therefore suspect. Fifty-one of the women he interviewed claimed that they found out that their husbands had been exposed to family violence in childhood and Gayford appeared anxious to make a link between violence in adult life and childhood to establish the existence of a generational "cycle of violence." The women were repeating what they had been told by their husbands or relatives of husbands, with little, if any, consideration of the time factor in memory involved at either end. Another fallacy of Gayford's study was his comparison of the battering husbands with the fathers of the women, attempting to suggest that women who had violent fathers grew up to marry brutal husbands. He did not bear this out in his own research with any evidence.

AMERICAN LITERATURE

At the same time that England focused its attention on the battered wife, America was focusing its attention on rape as a violent crime. Only within the past five years has America turned to focus on the battered woman. One American researcher has investigated the belief that violence passed on from generation to generation. Richard Gelles' study (1972) was the largest to date, although only eighty families were interviewed, where mostly wives and not husbands participated. Gelles claimed that "a common factor throughout the research on violent individuals is that they had a high level of physical brutality inflicted on them throughout childhood and adolescence." The informal interview lacked the sophistication of empirical methods of research, despite Gelles' explanations for choice of that method for his study. Gelles indicated that of the individuals he questioned who had observed violence between their own parents, fifty percent themselves engaged in violence, though he did not indicate to whom. He further indicated that only thirty percent of those who had not witnessed violence between their parents themselves engaged in violence. But these results leave questions. If violence was learned in the home why did fifty percent of the sample not engage in violence themselves? And why did thirty percent who had witnessed no violence in their childhood take to it? As Gelles himself admitted this hypothesis doesn't explain how much violence--examples given were often of very infrequent violence and are simply the adult's memories of childhood. Nevertheless Gelles felt confident enough to state that the home was a training ground for violence, learned by children from their parents. Freudian psychiatrists and psychologists have always maintained that children learn from those with whom they have an emotional relationship. In the last decade or so experimental and other psychologists have become interested in the whole question of how children learn and how they are "socialized"--i.e., how they are brought up--and have done a number of studies on imitation by children. It seems likely that children do indeed learn by copying adults, but they do not necessarily always copy their parents (Kennedy, 1971). Gelles' "common sense" explanation would seem an over-simplification, and children do not mechanically copy the nearest available "role model" of their sex. Not only may girls identify with fathers and boys with mothers, but there is a wide range of people outside the family who have a considerable influence on the way in which children adapt themselves.

Gelles, like Gayford, because of the practical difficulties and expense of finding battered women in the community at large by means of a random sample, based his research on a partially self-selected group: forty families referred by police and casework agencies "where known incidents of violence had taken place." But unlike Gayford, Gelles attempted to form a control group of forty similar families by means of random interviewing of neighbors of the known violent families. Also, unlike Gayford, he was cautious about the meaning that could be given his study: "In no way are the eighty individual family members we talked to representative of any population. . ." (Gelles, 1972:26). Gelles indicated that the small sample size inhibited full statistical testing of the quantitative data, creating a problem of inferring whether or not the relationships found were in fact true associations or occurred because of random factors. Gayford had no statistician to help with his research and there was no evidence that he understood the complex nature of statistical evidence.

Gayford is criticized for using a questionnaire method of getting his information, since it was suggested that the women did not always fill out their forms accurately. A questionnaire, as Gelles suggested, was not the best method of obtaining this sort of information. Gelles used the informal unstructured interview. Gayford freely admitted that his sample was biased. He left untouched certain seemingly vital areas in his research. He did not inquire into which women had had abortions, nor did he consider the question of bad housing conditions. Other researchers have commented on these factors, as well as unemployment, the wife's lack of special skills, the alcohol and immaturity factors. All that can be said about

Gayford's research in a positive sense is that it provided one of the earliest research studies at a time when the entire problem of wife-battering was also just coming to view. Any jump to conclusions that are made from his research would not only be premature, but also unsound.

Bean and Kerckhoff (1971) presented a study of personality and perceptions in husband-wife conflicts using sixty husbands and wives in a game situation where the participants were not aware of responding to a non-systematic response protocol supplied by the examiner; it was more specifically known as the Prisoner's Dilemma Game. The study was labeled as exploratory in nature, and no information was given about the sixty couples that participated, thus limiting the value in terms of the present study, other than to point out that both the wife and husband were involved in the attempt at this type of research.

In an article on communication, Dr. Leon Saul (1972) discussed personal and social psychopathology and the primary prevention of violence in terms of the perpetuation of pathology from childhood into adulthood. Saul believed that emotional disorders in parents are passed on mostly to the children, which tends to support Gayford's theory of the "cycle of violence." Saul presented an equation, stating that hostile aggression was not a constant force in human beings but varied among individuals. He represented it in a formula in which H = hostility, A = a tendency to act out, C = controls (conscious and unconscious), E = external forces, L = love, I = identification with others, and V = violent acting out, thus

$$\frac{H \times A \times E}{C \times L \times I} = V.$$ As H, A, and E increased and as C, L, and I decreased, V increased to pathological intensity. Unfortunately, the author did not offer any solution but stated that practical steps could be taken and coordinated in an effort to achieve national and international goals and purposes, which he did not even state.

Back in the Fifties sociology and psychology books about the family described it as the haven for all good feelings. But now it has been found that the supposedly warm and cozy home life was actually very violent. The Federal Bureau of Investigation reported that in 1969 a quarter of all murders took place within the family. The researchers Steinmetz and Strauss (1975) suggested that about as many people were murdered by their relatives in one six-month period in New York City as had been killed in three and one-half years of political upheaval in Northern Ireland. They also found that in those same cozy homes eighty-four to ninety-seven percent of parents were using corporal punishment as the primary means of discipline. Steinmetz and Strauss' book, <u>Violence in the Family</u>, was sociologically oriented, but contained many of their own original articles on violence as well as com- pilations upon violence between spouses and kin, violent parents, and the family as training ground for society's violence, supporting Gayford's "cycle of violence" theme.

In one of the few articles concerning battered wives, Marcella Schuyler (1976) discussed the problems of wives who were abused and brutalized by their husbands as one that has been largely ignored. She demonstrated in the article the isolation of the battered wife as a result of society's failure to assist in America, as did Erin Pizzey in England, and proposed strategies for dealing with wife abuse for social workers. Schuyler stated that at present, the problem of battered wives was being interpreted according to a number of unresearched assumptions. Schuyler went on to state that if a profile of the battered wife were determined, work toward prevention and the development of appropriate counseling approaches could begin. She concluded that encouragement of public discussion and research relating to the problem of battered wives was ultimately the foundation from which more sympathetic attitudes toward these women would evolve.

At the present time in America, few books about wife battering exist, and those that do each have their own bias. For example, while Del Martin's book (1976) was the most comprehensive, she infused it with a definite feminist slant. Martin dealt with the cultural and legal pressures battered wives have faced, and presented many examples of these problems. She offered her own solutions and suggestions as to what should be done, along with descriptions of what help was presently available. Martin, in relation to the psychological profession, provided a one-sided presentation, suggesting that "the clinician often adheres to the patriarchal myths that form our cultural heritage." She went on to suggest that if the woman seeking psychotherapy does not shop around and proceed with skepticism, she may find herself in the care of a therapist who subscribed to the theories of female inferiority and innate masochism and actually believed that a battered woman provoked and deserved the abuse she got. How realistic was she really being in terms of the needs of a woman in the battering situation for some kind of professional help? Martin's choice of psychological authorities obviously reflected her own bias. She encouraged battered women to seek out a feminist therapist. Nowhere in any literature or research has there been anything to support or disprove that in some cases the battered women may not invite or provoke her mate. On the positive side, Martin did compile and organize a comprehensive picture of the present situation in terms of social and legal organizations and avenues of help here in America.

The most recent book was written by Roger Langley and Richard C. Levy (1977), and alternated case study chapters with discussions of the problem, both socially and legally, as well as historically, through utilization of quotations from great literary works of the world. The authors both have a journalistic background, and drew much of their information from previously mentioned literature and research, as well as from informal interviews with medical and legal personnel, and social workers who were involved directly with the problem of wife-beating. Because of their detached involvement with the problem, the authors appeared to take a more objective approach than those who were directly involved with it. They made several unsubstantiated statements that would tend to mislead a layman; for example, they stated that there was hidden violence in at least a third of all American marriages. The book contained a chapter dealing with battered men, which was only briefly mentioned by Martin, and which was currently being investigated by sociologist Suzanne Steinmetz.

Several women's magazines such as the
Ladies' Home Journal and MS magazine have in
the past two years attempted to bring the problem of wife-beating into the open by publishing
articles aimed at encouraging women to bring
their problem to the attention of legal agencies. The Los Angeles television station
KABC-TV ran a week-long series in October 1977
and January 1978 aimed at the same goal, to
inform and make the public more aware of the
problem. The programs also encouraged support
for recent legislation designed to establish
several pilot program shelters in California
that would provide shelter for women adults and
their children, transportation, counseling, and
referrals for medical and legal help for battered wives. The legislature and many women's
organizations have been working to make changes
in the status of women in general and are attempting to get them to help themselves as well
as to seek help. As Schuyler indicated, it will
take an informed public to make lasting changes.

SUMMARY

Existent literature and research on wife-battering is both sparse and inconclusive,
mainly sociologically oriented, dealing with
the problem from within the familial context.
Most of the research studies are empirically
non-viable, drawing assumptions from self-constructed questionnaires and informal interviews and observations of one member of the
family. There has been little focus upon the
battered woman or the battering man, except in
research using those who have come into contact
with the legal system or some other social
agency, who may only prove to be the tip of the

iceberg, in terms of the entire spectrum in society. Clearly, a need for more empirical study and focus upon the individuals involved is needed, as mentioned by several of the researchers and writers.

CHAPTER 3

DESIGN AND PROCEDURE

This chapter contains the methods and procedures of the study. For the purpose presentation the chapter has been divided into five sections, namely, description of the null hypotheses, description of the subjects, description of the research instrumentation, description of the procedures, and treatment of the data.

NULL HYPOTHESES

The hypotheses of the study stated in the null form are as follows:

1. There is no significant difference (p .05) between battered and non-battered wife personality characteristics as measured by the Sixteen Personality Factor Questionnaire.

2. There is no significant difference between battered and non-battered wife personality profiles as measured by the Sixteen Personality Factor Questionnaire.

3. There is no significant difference (p .05) between battered and non-battered wife self-concept factors as measured by the Tennessee Self Concept Scale.

4. There is no significant difference between battered and non-battered wife self-concept profiles as measured by the Tennessee Self Concept Scale.

SUBJECTS

Subjects were obtained from within the San Bernardino County, and consisted of sixty women who had been or were presently involved in a marital relationship, either legal or common-law. The sixty women made up two groups of thirty each; one group consisted of women who had been battered, the other group consisted of women who had never been battered by their husbands. Subjects were considered on the basis of criteria that follow.

Adult females who had been beaten on more than one occasion by their mates to the degree that medical attention was warranted, or which could be witnessed upon her person. All subjects had completed the eighth grade; some had attended college. Forty-six were presently living with the battering spouse at the time of testing. They had been married an average of ten years. There was an average of two children in the home. Fifty-five of the spouses were employed. The age range was from 16 to 64 years. The ethnic breakdown consisted of three Mexican Americans, two Black Americans, one Oriental, and 54 Caucasians of various descent. All subjects were volunteers from within the community setting; none were or had received any professional help for their marital difficulties or the problem of wife-battering. Forty-three subjects were obtained through referral from acquaintances and/or friends; twelve were obtained through advertising in the local free press, and five from signs in women's restrooms. The ads and signs stated, "Are you a battered wife? Call 862-2940. Confidential." Permission had been obtained from the managers of the two main shopping centers in San Bernardino to post the signs in their public restrooms. One battering husband answered the press advertisement, worded as above, and was referred to a local agency for counseling. Additional descriptive material can be found in Appendix A.

Possible subjects were screened by the researcher in a face-to-face informal interview. The time and place was set for testing to be done at a later date. Battered women were so designated only by their own self-report; evidence of recent battering was visible in nineteen of the thirty battered subjects; one battered woman was interviewed in the hospital, where she had been since her last battering only hours before contact. Evidence of prior battering was present in the form of bruises, scars, burns, and similar marks. Twelve initial contacts were made by phone with battered wives, who then failed to appear for the interview. None of the women who did appear for the interview failed to follow through with the testing. Most of the battered women contacted were initially afraid that their spouses would find out about their participation. Anonymity was assured throughout the entire process by coding of answer sheets and use of first names in all contacts.

INSTRUMENTATION

Two self-report questionnaires were used in the study. The questionnaires used were the Sixteen Personality Factor Questionnaire

(Cattell, et al., 1970), and the Tennessee Self Concept Scale (Fitts, 1965). Both instruments met the defined dimensions of characteristics and self-concept, criteria, and behavioral factors previously specified in Chapter 1.

Sixteen Personality
Factor Questionnaire
(16PF) Form A

The 16PF is a multifactor personality trait dimension measurement instrument consisting of 16 scales, presented in Chapter 1 and Table 1. The questionnaire measures 15 primary personality source traits and one intelligence measure. The 16PF, Form A, is composed of 187 items, which include 3 items to insure the respondent understands and answers all questions. The trait characteristics are expressed in nonpathological terminology based on standard scores called stens, calculated from the raw scores. Reading level of Form A is that of ordinary newspaper literate adults, and takes an average of 50 minutes to complete. The instrument has the advantage of nearly twenty-five years of extensive research, both theoretical and practical, and provides a comprehensive scheme aimed at mapping the whole area of personality behavior with factor analyzed items in a questionnaire of economical length, with the personality profile plotted on the back of the answer sheet itself. The 16PF has the advantage of greater reliability, including less subjectivity in scoring, than the Rorschach and Thematic Apperception Test (Buros, 1972) and satisfactorily estimated reliabilities and validities as listed in Table 1, which follows. Directions for administration are contained

Table 1

Sixteen Personality Factor Questionnaire - Form A

	Characteristic	Reliability*	Direct Validity**
A	Reserved-Outgoing	.81	.79
B	Less-More Intelligent	.58	.35
C	Affected by Feelings-Emotionally Stable	.78	.70
E	Humble-Assertive	.80	.63
F	Sober-Happy-go-lucky	.79	.83
G	Expedient-Conscientious	.81	.67
H	Shy-Venturesome	.83	.92
I	Toughminded-Tenderminded	.77	.70
L	Trusting-Suspicious	.75	.49
M	Practical-Imaginative	.70	.44
N	Forthright-Shrewd	.61	.41
O	Self-Assured-Apprehensive	.79	.71
Q_1	Conservative-Experimenting	.73	.62
Q_2	Group Dependent-Self-sufficient	.73	.70
Q_3	Undisciplined Self Conflict-Control	.62	.68
Q_4	Tense-Relaxed	.81	.57

*Reliability of dependent variables is based on test-retest with 146 American subjects - 79 employment counselors and 67 undergraduate college students - over a four to seven day period (Cattell, 1970).

**Direct Validity for Form A for each factor scale based on a standardization number of 958 (Cattell, 1970).

within the booklet itself, making the questionnaire self-administering.

Tennessee Self Concept Scale (TSCS)

The TSCS consists of one hundred self descriptive statements which subjects used to portray their own pictures of themselves. Of the 100 items, ten comprise the self-criticism scale. The other ninety items measure the several components of self-concept and are equally divided into 45 positive and 45 negative statements in an attempt to minimize the bias of a positive or negative response set. The TSCS provides a multi-dimensional description of self-concept, which is listed in Chapter 1 and in Table 2, with indicated levels of reliability. In a study based on 102 psychiatric patients, correlations were studied between all profile variables on the TSCS and all scales on the Minnesota Multiphasic Personality Inventory. Using Pearson's correlation, ratios ranged from -.64 to .68 (Fitts, 1965). Two criteria were set in establishing validity. One is content validity, based on the assumption that the categories used in the Scale are logically meaningful and publicly communicable; an item was retained in the Scale only if there was unanimous agreement by the judges that it was classified correctly. It was determined that the classification system used for the Row Scores and Column Scores was dependable by assumption. The other approach was whether the Scale differentiated between groups. Statistical analyses were performed in which a large group (369) of psychiatric patients were compared with 626 non-patients of a norm group. Highly significant (mostly at the .001 level)

Table 2

Tennessee Self Concept Scale

Factor	Reliability*
1. The Total Concept Self	.92
1.1 The Identity	.91
1.2 Self Satisfaction	.88
1.3 Behavior	.88
1.4 Physical Self	.87
1.5 Moral-ethical Self	.85
1.6 Personal Self	.85
1.7 Family Self	.89
1.8 Social Self	.90
1.9 Self Criticism	.75
2. Defensive Positive	.90
3. General Maladjustment	.87
4. Psychotic	.92
5. Personality Disorder	.90
6. Neurotic	.91
7. Personality Integration	.89

*Reliability of the dependent variables based on test-retest of 60 college students over a two-week period (Fitts, 1965).

differences between patients and non-patients for almost every score were achieved. Administration time for the TSCS is relatively short, about twenty minutes, using standardized instructions. The Tennessee Self Concept Scale can be used with persons who read at the sixth grade reading level.

PROCEDURE

The 16PF and TSCS were given to 60 women under standard instructions, in individual sessions with each subject. The TSCS was administered first, followed by the 16PF during the same session. Subjects took varying amounts of time to complete the questionnaires with most completing both in less than one and one half hours. All questionnaires were administered from January 17 to August 30, 1977.

Subjects were instructed to read the instructions contained in the booklet for the TSCS, and allowed to ask questions if they desired regarding the instructions. The same procedure was followed regarding the 16PF. Emphasis was made upon the importance of responding to all questions, choosing the response most likely to be chosen when the subject was not completely sure the description fit her.

The Tennessee Self Concept Scale was scored by computer, while the Sixteen Personality Factor Questionnaire was hand-scored, so that an individual profile could also be completed. Hand-scored answers were triple-checked, to ensure accuracy. All answer sheets were number-coded to provided anonymity.

Raw scores were converted to stens from norm tables in Tabular Supplement No. 1 to the 16PF Handbook (1970), before plotting individual personality profiles on the reverse side of the answer sheets. All statistical procedures were run via computer for each questionnaire and for both groups of wives.

DATA ANALYSIS

Kerlinger indicates that "there is no better way to study research design than through an analysis of variance approach," (Kerlinger, 1973:221) suggesting that analysis of variance is what its name implies--and more: a method of identifying, breaking down, and testing for statistical significance variances that come from different sources of variation. All data collected relative to personality characteristics and self-concept factors of battered and non-battered wives was analyzed by a one-way analysis of variance, in keeping with Hypothesis 1, 2, 3 and 4.

T-tests were computed for the demographic variables of years of education, age at which first married, number of marriages, number of children, total family income, and age of wives. Chi square analyses were computed for present marital status, and whether the woman was presently working.

Results of the above statistical procedures will be presented in tabular and figure form in Chapter 4.

CHAPTER 4

RESULTS

The results of the study are presented in five parts. The first section is concerned with the testing of Hypothesis 1 in the null form and involves determining whether or not the personality characteristics of the Sixteen Personality Factor Questionnaire show a significant difference between battered and non-battered wives.

The second section is concerned with testing of Hypothesis 2 in the null form and involves determining whether or not the personality profiles of battered and non-battered wives show a significant difference.

The third section is concerned with the testing of Hypothesis 3 in the null form and involves determining whether or not the self-concept factors of the Tennessee Self Concept Scale show a significant difference between the battered and non-battered wives.

The fourth section is concerned with testing of Hypothesis 4 in the null form and involves determining whether or not the self-concept profiles of battered and non-battered wives show a significant difference. The fifth section is concerned with additional results and comparisons.

HYPOTHESIS 1--NULL FORM

There is no significant difference ($p<.05$) between battered and non-battered wife personality characteristics as measured by the Sixteen Personality Factor Questionnaire.

Table 3 represents a summary of the analysis of variance of personality characteristics of battered and non-battered wife groups, indicating between-group mean squares, variance, and identification of significant characteristics for the thirty battered and the thirty non-battered wife subjects. Four characteristics are found to be significant. The characteristic indicative of ego strength (Affected by Feelings-Emotionally Stable), was highly significant ($p<.001$) in the battered wife group, signifying individuals affected by feelings, emotionally less stable, easily upset and changeable, who suffer their maladjustment as internal conflict. The trait characteristic, Self-assured-Apprehension is highly significant ($p<.001$) in the battered wife group, indicative of guilt proneness, apprehension, self-reproachment, insecurity, worrying, and being generally troubled. The characteristic, Undisciplined Self-conflict-Controlled is found significant ($p<.05$) in the battered group, indicating low self-sentiment integration, a tendency to be uncontrolled and lax following own urges, and carelessness of social rules. The characteristic, Relaxed-Tense was found highly significant ($p<.001$) in the battered wife group, indicative of frustrated, driven, overwrought, and fretful individuals, in which the "id" energy is misdirected, or converted into psychosomatic disturbances, generally disruptive of steady application and emotional balance. The findings justify

Table 3

Summary of Analysis of Variance of Personality
Characteristics of Battered and Non-Battered Wives

Characteristics	Between-Group Mean^2	Variance	$F(df59)=4.01$ $(p<.05)$
Reserved-Outgoing	13.07	2.62	
Less-More Intelligent	0.60	.21	
Lower-Higher Ego Strength	74.82	28.17	**
Humble-Assertive	2.02	.44	
Sober-Happy-go-lucky	0.82	.13	
Expedient-Conscientious	2.02	.45	
Shy-Venturesome	19.27	3.05	
Tough-Tender-minded	4.82	2.11	
Trusting-Suspicious	6.67	2.26	
Practical-Imaginative	0.15	.04	
Forthright-Astute	2.02	.54	
Self-assured-Apprehensive	117.60	35.01	**
Conservative-Experimenting	15.00	3.62	
Group dependent-Self-sufficient	0.60	.11	
Undisciplined Self-conflict-Controlled	26.67	5.46	*
Relaxed-Tense	72.60	36.26	**

*Significant at .05 level.
**Significant at .01 level.

accepting the research hypothesis and rejecting the statistical (null) hypothesis.

HYPOTHESIS 2--NULL FORM

There is no significant difference between battered and non-battered wife personality profiles as measured by the Sixteen Personality Factor Questionnaire.

Figure 1 presents the summary personality profile of the battered wife and the non-battered wives. Four of the sixteen characteristics are found to be significantly different. The battered wife group is more affected by feelings, more apprehensive, has undisciplined self conflict, and is more tense than the non-battered group. The findings justify rejecting the statistical (null) hypothesis and accepting the research hypothesis.

HYPOTHESIS 3--NULL FORM

There is no significant difference ($p<.05$) between battered and non-battered wife self-concept factors as measured by the Tennessee Self Concept Scale.

Table 4 presents a summary of the analysis of variance of self-concept factors of battered and non-battered wife groups, indicating between-group mean squares, the variance, and identification of significant factors for the thirty battered and the thirty non-battered wife subjects. Fifteen of the self-concept factors were found to be highly significant ($p<.001$). The self-criticism factor was found to be non-significant. The battered wife group was found to have lower self-esteem, and more difficulty

Figure 1

Summary Personality Profile of Battered
and Non-Battered Wives

X Battered (N=30)
O Non-Battered (N=30)

LOW SCORE DESCRIPTION	STANDARD TEN SCORE (STEN) Low — Average — High 1 2 3 4 (5 6) 7 8 9 10	HIGH SCORE DESCRIPTION
RESERVED, DETACHED, CRITICAL, ALOOF, STIFF (Sizothymia)		OUTGOING, WARMHEARTED, EASY-GOING, PARTICIPATING (Affectothymia)
LESS INTELLIGENT, CONCRETE-THINKING (Lower scholastic mental capacity)		MORE INTELLIGENT, ABSTRACT-THINKING, BRIGHT (Higher scholastic mental capacity)
AFFECTED BY FEELINGS, EMOTIONALLY LESS STABLE, EASILY UPSET, CHANGEABLE (Lower ego strength)		EMOTIONALLY STABLE, MATURE, FACES REALITY, CALM (Higher ego strength)
HUMBLE, MILD, EASILY LED, DOCILE, ACCOMMODATING (Submissiveness)		ASSERTIVE, AGGRESSIVE, STUBBORN, COMPETITIVE (Dominance)
SOBER, TACITURN, SERIOUS (Desurgency)		HAPPY-GO-LUCKY, ENTHUSIASTIC (Surgency)
EXPEDIENT, DISREGARDS RULES (Weaker superego strength)		CONSCIENTIOUS, PERSISTENT, MORALISTIC, STAID (Stronger superego strength)
SHY, TIMID, THREAT-SENSITIVE (Threctia)		VENTURESOME, UNINHIBITED, SOCIALLY BOLD (Parmia)
TOUGH-MINDED, SELF-RELIANT, REALISTIC (Harria)		TENDER-MINDED, SENSITIVE, CLINGING, OVERPROTECTED (Premsia)
TRUSTING, ACCEPTING CONDITIONS (Alaxia)		SUSPICIOUS, HARD TO FOOL (Protension)
PRACTICAL, "DOWN-TO-EARTH" CONCERNS (Praxernia)		IMAGINATIVE, BOHEMIAN, ABSENT-MINDED (Autia)
FORTHRIGHT, UNPRETENTIOUS, GENUINE BUT SOCIALLY CLUMSY (Artlessness)		ASTUTE, POLISHED, SOCIALLY AWARE (Shrewdness)
SELF-ASSURED, PLACID, SECURE, COMPLACENT, SERENE (Untroubled adequacy)		APPREHENSIVE, SELF-REPROACHING, INSECURE, WORRYING, TROUBLED (Guilt proneness)
CONSERVATIVE, RESPECTING TRADITIONAL IDEAS (Conservatism of temperament)		EXPERIMENTING, LIBERAL, FREE-THINKING (Radicalism)
GROUP-DEPENDENT, A "JOINER" AND SOUND FOLLOWER (Group adherence)		SELF-SUFFICIENT, RESOURCEFUL, PREFERS OWN DECISIONS (Self-sufficiency)
UNDISCIPLINED SELF-CONFLICT, LAX, FOLLOWS OWN URGES, CARELESS OF SOCIAL RULES (Low integration)		CONTROLLED, EXACTING WILL POWER, SOCIALLY PRECISE, COMPULSIVE (High strength of self-sentiment)
RELAXED, TRANQUIL, UNFRUSTRATED, COMPOSED (Low ergic tension)		TENSE, FRUSTRATED, DRIVEN, OVERWROUGHT (High ergic tension)

A sten of 1   2   3   4   (5   6)   7   8   9   10 is obtained
by about 2.3% 4.4% 9.2% 15.0% 19.1% 19.1% 15.0% 9.2% 4.4% 2.3% of adults

© 1973

Copyright © 1956, 1973, by the Institute for Personality
and Ability Testing, Inc. All rights reserved. Reprinted
by permission of the copyright owner.

39

Table 4

Summary of Analysis of Variance of Self-Concept
Factors of Battered and Non-Battered Wives

Factor	Between-Group Mean^2	Variance	$F(df\ 59)-4.01$ $(p<.05)$
Self-criticism	12.13	.11	
Total Self-esteem	5568.06	30.26	**
Identity	6427.37	27.71	**
Self-satisfaction	4018.06	24.57	**
Behavior	3856.00	24.14	**
Physical self	3760.44	15.06	**
Moral-ethical self	3542.00	20.45	**
Personal self	4576.25	26.64	**
Family self	6161.12	29.89	**
Social self	2926.06	18.59	**
Defensive positive	1392.00	15.62	**
General maladjustment	6060.19	32.78	**
Psychosis	2196.19	13.11	**
Personality disorder	2535.00	19.60	**
Neurosis	4489.81	26.39	**
Personality integration	1066.81	8.74	**

*Significant at .05 level.
**Significant at .01 level.

with basic identity. The battered wife group appears to be less satisfied with itself in terms of its own behavior, physical self, moral-ethical self, family self, social self, and appears to have difficulty maintaining minimal self-esteem, as indicated by the defensive positive factor. As a group, the battered wives appear to be generally more maladjusted, with higher scores on psychosis, personality disorder, and neurosis factors. The group shows overall less integration of personality when compared with the non-battered group. The findings justify accepting the research hypothesis and rejecting the statistical (null) hypothesis.

HYPOTHESIS 4--NULL FORM

There is no significant difference between battered and non-battered wife self-concept profiles as measured by the Tennessee Self Concept Scale.

Figure 2 presents a summary profile of the self-concept factors of the battered wife and non-battered wife groups. All but one of the factors are found to be significantly different; that factor is self-criticism. The findings justify accepting the research hypothesis and rejecting the statistical (null) hypothesis.

ADDITIONAL RESULTS

During the computation phase of the study with the Sixteen Personality Factor Questionnaire, it was felt that the second order and derivative scores would be of value in light of the results of the analysis of variance of first order scores. Three of the six were found to be significant.

Figure 2

Summary Profile Sheet

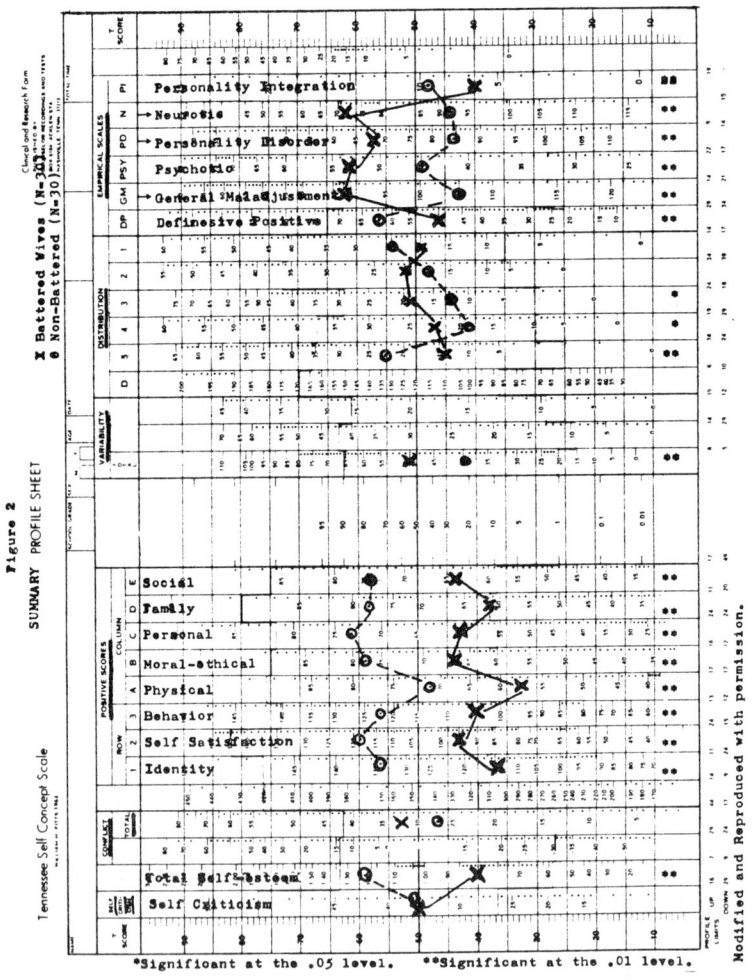

Table 5 presents a summary of the analysis of variance of the second order and derivative characteristics of the Sixteen Personality Factor Questionnaire results for the battered wife and non-battered wife groups.

The anxiety factor was found to be highly significant (p<.001) in the battered wife group. This score has been found to be usually very high in neurotics, but in itself is not considered pathological. The high significance of the neuroticism characteristic coupled with

Table 5

Summary of Analysis of Variance of Second Order and Derivative Characteristics of the 16PF for Battered and Non-Battered Wives

Characteristic	Between-Group Mean^2	Variance	$F(df59)=4.01$ (p<.05)
Extraversion	4.53	.85	
Anxiety	99.33	57.61	**
Tough Poise	5.64	2.06	
Independence	0.75	.21	
Neuroticism	62.62	22.15	**
Leadership	48.61	14.50	**

**Significant at the .01 level.

anxiety suggests strong neurotic tendencies. The leadership characteristic was found to be significant in battered wife group, indicating an individual who is less likely to become a leader.

During the computation phase of the study with the Tennessee Self Concept Scale, seven additional scores were computed in order to present a self-concept profile.

Table 6 presents the additional TSCS factors for battered and non-battered wife groups. A summary of the analysis of variance of the factors with between-group mean squares and variance, as well as indication of significant factors for both groups is shown.

Total variability was found to be highly significant, suggesting that battered wife group had self concepts so variable from one area to another as to reflect little unity or integration. This is additionally substantiated by the significance of three distribution scores of the battered wives suggesting subjects who are very indefinite and uncertain about the way they perceive themselves. Two other distribution scores were not found significant. No significant difference in the total amount of conflict without regard to the nature or direction of the conflict was found.

SUMMARY

The results of the study were presented in five basic parts. The first section was concerned with the testing of Hypothesis 1 in the null form and involved determining if there was a significant difference between battered and

Table 6

Summary of Analysis of Variance of Additional Factors of the TSCS for Battered and Non-Battered Wives

Factor	Between-Group Mean^2	Variance	$F(df59)=4.01$ $(p<.05)$
Total Conflict	481.69	3.54	
Total Variability	1325.37	14.69	**
Distribution - 5	2500.00	10.53	**
Distribution - 4	448.25	5.19	*
Distribution - 3	693.56	4.95	*
Distribution - 2	273.06	1.82	
Distribution - 1	400.38	2.89	

*Significant at the .05 level.
**Significant at the .01 level.

non-battered wife personality characteristics as measured by the Sixteen Personality Factor Questionnaire. The findings justified acceptance of the research hypothesis and rejection of the statistical (null) hypothesis.

The second section was concerned with testing of Hypothesis 2 in the null form and involved determining whether or not the personality profiles of battered and non-battered wives showed a significant difference as measured by the Sixteen Personality Factor Questionnaire. The findings justified acceptance of the research hypothesis and rejection of the statistical (null) hypothesis.

The third section was concerned with the testing of Hypothesis 3 in the null form and involved determining whether or not the self-concept factors of the Tennessee Self Concept Scale showed a significant difference between the battered and non-battered wives. The findings justified acceptance of the research hypothesis and rejection of the statistical (null) hypothesis.

The fourth section was concerned with testing of Hypothesis 4 in the null form and involved determining whether or not the self-concept profiles of battered and non-battered wives showed a significant difference as measured by the Tennessee Self Concept Scale. The findings justified acceptance of the research hypothesis and rejection of the statistical (null) hypothesis.

The fifth section was concerned with additional results not originally planned for. Second order and derivative scores were computer-run for the Sixteen Personality Factor Questionnaire. Of the six additional characteristics, three were found to be highly significant (.01), including anxiety, neuroticism, and leadership. Extraversion, tough poise, and independence were not found significant. Additional scores were computer-run for the Tennessee Self Concept Scale. Of the seven factors, four were found to be significant. These included total variability of self-concept, and three of the five distribution scores. Total conflict and two distribution factors were not found to be significant.

CHAPTER 5

DISCUSSION, CONCLUSIONS AND RECOMMENDATIONS

This section is concerned with the discussion of the findings of the study and implications for further research. The delimitations and assumptions listed in Chapter 1 bear upon the discussion and recommendations.

DISCUSSION

The findings of the study led to the following conclusions:

1. Battered wives fall at the lower limits of ego strength, whereas non-battered wives fall at the middle or average range of the Sixteen Personality Factor Profile.

2. Battered wives and non-battered wives maintain approximately the same average range of superego strength on the Sixteen Personality Factor Questionnaire.

3. Battered wives score significantly higher than non-battered wives on the Apprehensive characteristic of the 16PF profile.

4. Battered wives score significantly lower than non-battered wives in Undisciplined Self-Conflict and Integration on the 16PF profile.

5. Battered wives evidence significantly higher ergic tension than non-battered wives.

6. Battered wives show lower self-esteem and more difficulty with basic identity than non-battered wives on the Tennessee Self Concept Scale.

7. Battered wives were less satisfied with themselves in terms of their behavior, physical self, moral-ethical self, family self, social self, and have more difficulty maintaining minimal self-esteem than non-battered wives.

8. Wives who have been battered are generally more maladjusted, with overall less integration of personality than non-battered wives.

CONCLUSIONS

The first conclusion would be consistent with Cattell's (1970) contention that an individual would tend to be more uncontrolled, disorganized, generally emotional, with a proneness to get into fights and problem situations because the person becomes easily annoyed by things and people, is dissatisfied with the world situation, her family, the restrictions of life, health, and feels unable to cope with life, when showing a lack of integration and maturity of ego strength. Esyenck (1953) indicated that "general neuroticism" would be characteristic to this type of orientation, though later research (Cattell, 1973) shows these features present in all kinds of clinical disorders.

The second conclusion suggests that all of the subjects have a normal deeply-rooted concern for moral standards, tend to put forth persistent effort, and in general, tend to drive the ego and to restrain the id impulses in a somewhat consistent manner. Cattell (1970) suggests this factor deals with attitudes implanted early by strong fear and affection, and that they are partly unconscious and no longer subject to rational manipulation, stemming from early childhood training.

The third conclusion conforms with the concept that clinically, apprehension is one of the largest factors in anxiety (Cattell, 1970), with high guilt proneness, self-reproachment, insecurity, and worrying as accompanying features. These are important indicators of unstable, overexcitable individuals who feel inadequate to meet the daily demands of life, and tend to become easily downhearted and remorseful. These factors are commonly found in neurotics, alcoholics, and many psychotics (Cattell, Tatro, and Komlos, 1964, 1965). The characteristic is considered to be one of long-term stress, not necessarily changeable with the situation, or influenced by the nourishing or depleting elements of the environment, but rather existing due to an underlying, long-term tension state and thus is more difficult to change.

The fourth conclusion of low self-sentiment and integration is representative of the strength of the individual's concern about his self-concept and social image (Cattell, 1970). It represents the level of development of the conscious, behavior-integrating self-sentiment, suggesting here that battered wives have lost concern about and regard for attainment of an ideal pattern of self of socially approved behavior to which the individual normally makes attempts to conform. The characteristic has been called by G. F. Stice (Cattell and Stice, 1954) the "gyroscopic" factor in the personality in its role of aiding integration.

The fifth conclusion indicates that wives who have been battered evidence high general ergic energy excited in excess of the ego strength capacity to discharge it, so it is misdirected, or converted into psychosomatic disturbances and anxiety, and is generally disruptive of steady application and emotional balance. It is a significant factor in the differentiation of neurotics from normals (Cattell, 1970), and is representative of situational tension rather than that related to long-term stress. Clinically it can be expressed as representing a level of excitement and tension, expressing undischarged and poorly controllable "libido."

The sixth conclusion reveals that women who have been battered show greater total conflict within themselves and lower self-esteem, indicative of general confusion, contradiction, and general conflict in self perception. The conflict scores are considered reflections of conflicting responses to positive and negative items within the same area of self perception, whereas the identity score is where the individual is describing her own basic identity-- i.e., what she is as she sees herself (Fitts, 1965). The lack of significance found in the self-criticism score may be deceptive, in that low scores can be an indication of defensiveness, or an inability to accept negative concepts of herself when forced into a situation where she must be self-critical.

The seventh conclusion indicates that battered wives have much less satisfaction with themselves as opposed to non-battered wives. All elements of the self, including behavior, physical self, moral-ethical self, family self, and social self, were found to be highly significant. The behavior factor is a measure of the individual's perception of her own behavior or the way she functions (Fitts, 1965). Battered wives were highly unsatisfied with their own bodies, their state of health, physical appearance, skills and sexuality. They had a great deal of dissatisfaction, in addition, with their own moral worth, their relationship to God, their feelings of being a "good" or "bad" person, and their satisfaction with their religion or lack of it. The wives who have been battered have a low sense of personal worth, feelings of inadequacy as a person, and a poor evaluation of their personality apart from their body, and their relationship to others. Battered wives reflect feelings of inadequacy, worthlessness, and little or no value as a family member, compared with non-battered wives. In relation to the individual's overall sense of adequacy and worth in her social interaction with other people in general, battered wives were found to be significantly more dissatisfied with themselves at the .01 level, when compared with non-battered wives. The Defensive Positive Scale was very significant for battered wives, indicative of much difficulty in maintaining minimal self-esteem.

The final conclusion is that battered wives were found to be significantly more generally maladjusted. All of the maladjustment scales were significant at the .01 level, as indicated below. The psychosis scale differentiates psychotic patients from other groups (Fitts, 1965), while the personality disorder category pertains to people with basic personality defects and weaknesses in contrast to psychotic states or the various neurotic reactions. A highly significant score was found on the neurosis scale for the battered wives, correlating with the several characteristics of the 16PF that were found significant, and the second order 16PF Neurotic score. The wives who have been battered reflected less personality integration when compared to non-battered wives, to a very significant degree.

Because all of the wives who had been battered were known to be functioning within the community setting and within their own family situation, and were not receiving counseling or psychological help or were institutionalized at the inception of the study, the amount of maladjustment may seem to be misleading. Of the four personality characteristics found to be very significant, three are known to be factors that are of long-standing within the personality constellation, while only one factor would tend to be influenced by an immediate situational stress (Cattell, 1970). In addition, the large number of highly significant factors of the self-concept of the battered wife serves to confirm the poor state of mental health and general personality make-up. Fitts suggests that those who see themselves as undesirable, worthless, or "bad" tend to act accordingly, or unrealistically, adding to the concern for removing the battered wife from the battering situation.

All of the conclusions discussed confirm that wives who have been battered are more psychologically unhealthy than wives who have not been battered. Battered wives evidence significant differences in personality characteristics and self-concept factors from non-battered wives.

RECOMMENDATIONS

Further studies into the background of the battered wife and the marital relationship itself would be helpful in determining what the relationship of being battered is to the overall personality development of the individual and the interactions with a mate.

Additional research with larger samples and added variables comparing the battered wife and the non-battered wife is needed to determine how battering relates to personality differences within differing strata of society.

Studies of the battering husband's personality and self-concept would be helpful in determining what specific aspects may have a relationship to battering. The studies should be done with large samples in differing geographical areas and social situations and should be extended to comparisons of type of violence, frequency, family background of the husband, and such factors as alcoholism, drug usage, smoking, health, general economic and job factors, and attitudes.

Comparative studies should be initiated of battered wives who are in a shelter situation and those who are in the community at large. A test-retest basis should be considered to determine the effectiveness of removal from the battering situation, and the efficacy of any treatment plan that may be operative within the shelter environment and/or the community.

Family constellation studies using such instruments as Cattell's which cover a wide age range, would be helpful in determining a family profile of personality characteristics to determine their effect upon the interactions of family members. This data would facilitate planning a treatment approach designed for the family's specific needs, and should include all members of an immediate family able to respond to a testing instrument.

Studies of battered women who batter their own children would be helpful in determining the existence of any personality characteristics that might directly relate to the battering of their children. The development of a preventive program within the community, as well as treatment plans for the removal of relevant factors would be of benefit.

Development of a nuclear family study plan could provide important information if initiated with a battering family as the center of the constellation. Identification of significant factors through utilization of selected psychological instruments could help in developing a family profile related to violence.

SUMMARY

The issue of psychodiagnosis of battered wives has not been widely researched. There have been broad myths and unsubstantiated assumptions dealing with the etiology of the self-concept and personality characteristics of wives who have been battered and the determination of what factors may be significant within the personality constellation.

The purpose of this research was to identify specific personality characteristics and self-concept factors of wives who have been battered. The Sixteen Personality Factor Questionnaire and the Tennessee Self Concept Scale have been validated as reliable measures of personality characteristics and self-concept factors (Cattell, 1970; Fitts, 1965). However, the problem remained to develop a personality profile and a self-concept profile that would show any differences between battered wives and non-battered wives using the 16PF and TSCS data.

Similar studies have been done with the Sixteen Personality Factor Questionnaire using other categories such as occupational groups and clinical groups (Cattell, 1970).

A number of studies have been completed which study the relationship between self-concept and behavior (Fitts, 1965). Atchison (1958) found a number of predicted differences between delinquents and non-delinquents, while Lefeber (1964) found significant differences between juvenile first offenders and repeated offenders.

In a study of unwed mothers, Boston and Kew (1964) found predicted differences on virtually every variable of the Scale. Gividen (1959) found a number of scores which differentiated soldiers who could weather the stresses of paratrooper training from those who could not. Wells and Bueno (1957) found that a group of alcoholics had significantly low Positive scores, high Variability scores, and more extreme Distribution scores. Piety (1958) found that Total Positive scores discriminated patients from nonpatients at the .005 level, while a later, more extensive analysis of his data led him to make a blind patient, non-patient classification with seventy-two percent accuracy (p less than .001) (Fitts, 1965).

METHOD

To determine personality characteristics and self-concept factors, and develop profiles of battered wives, a total sample of N=60 was given the Sixteen Personality Factor Questionnaire and the Tennessee Self Concept Scale. Individual sample groups were as given: battered wives N-30, and non-battered wives N-30.

Hypothesis 1

Battered wives evidence different personality characteristics from non-battered wives as measured by the Sixteen Personality Factor Questionnaire.

A one-way analysis of variance was used to test Hypothesis 1 in the null form, and the level of significance was set at .05.

Hypothesis 2

Wives who have been battered evidence a different personality profile from non-battered wives as measured by the Sixteen Personality Factor Questionnaire.

A one-way analysis of variance was used to test Hypothesis 2 in the null form, and the level of significance was set at .05.

Hypothesis 3

There is a significant difference between the self-concept factors of battered wives and non-battered wives as measured by the Tennessee Self Concept Scale.

A one-way analysis of variance was used to test Hypothesis 3 in the null form, and the level of significance was set at .05.

Hypothesis 4

Wives who have been battered evidence a different self-concept profile from non-battered wives as measured by the Tennessee Self Concept Scale.

A one-way analysis of variance was used to test Hypothesis 4 in the null form, and the level of significance was set at .05.

RESULTS

The findings justified accepting Hypothesis 1 based on a rejection of the null form of this hypothesis at the .05 level of significance. There was a significant finding (.05) for one of the sixteen characteristics, and a highly significant finding (.001) for three other of the sixteen characteristics.

The findings justified accepting Hypothesis 2 based on a rejection of the null form of this hypothesis at the .05 level of significance. There was significant finding (.05 or less) on four of the sixteen characteristics.

The findings justified accepting Hypothesis 3 based on a rejection of the null form of this hypothesis at the .05 level of significance. Fifteen of the sixteen self-concept factors were significant; there was a very significant finding (.01) for five of the sixteen factors, and a highly significant finding (.001) for the other ten of the sixteen factors.

The findings justified accepting Hypothesis 4 based on a rejection of the null form of this hypothesis at the .05 level of significance. Only one of the sixteen factors was not significant.

Additional Results

In a summary of the one-way analysis of variance of second order and derivative characteristics of the Sixteen Personality Factor Questionnaire for battered and non-battered wives, three of the six characteristics were found to be very significant at the .01 level.

In a summary of the one-way analysis of variance of seven additional factors of the Tennessee Self Concept Scale for battered and non-battered wives, two factors were found to be significant at the .05 level, while two other factors were very significant at the .01 level.

BIBLIOGRAPHY

REFERENCES

Atchison, Calvin. 1958. "A Comparative Study of the Self-Concept of Behavior Problem and Non-Behavior Problem High School Boys." Unpublished Doctoral dissertation, Indiana University.

Bean, Frank D. and Alan C. Kerckhoff. 1971. "Personality and Perception in Husband-Wife Conflicts," Journal of Marriage and the Family, 33(2): 351-359.

Bloom, B. S. 1964. Stability and Changes in Human Characteristics. New York: John Wiley and Sons, Inc.

Boston, Geneva N. and Katherine L. Kew. 1964. "The Self Concept of the Unmarried Mother in the Florence Crittendon Home, Nashville, Tennessee." Unpublished master's thesis. Nashville: University of Tennessee.

Braun, John R. and Dolore La Faro. 1969. "Faking and Faking Detection on the 16PF Form A," Journal of Psychology. 71(2): 155-158.

Bruning, James L. and B. L. Kintz. 1968. Computational Handbook of Statistics. Glenview, Illinois: Scott, Foresman and Company.

Buros, O., ed. 1972. The Seventh Mental Measurements Yearbook. Highland Park, New Jersey: Gryphon Press.

Cattell, Raymond B. 1965. The Scientific Analysis of Personality. Chicago: Aldine Publishing Company.

_____. 1972. "The 16PF and Basic Personality Structure: A Reply to Esyenck," Journal of Behavioral Science. 1(4): 169-187.

_____. 1973. "Personality Pinned Down," Psychology Today. July: 40-46.

_____ and L. S. Bolton. 1969. "What Pathological Dimensions Lie Behind the Normal Dimensions of the 16PF?", Journal of Consulting and Clinical Psychology. 33: 18-29.

_____ and H. W. Eber. 1957. The Sixteen Personality Questionnaire. Champaign, Illinois, Institute for Personality and Ability Testing.

_____, Herbert W. Eber and Maurice M. Tatsuoka. 1970. Handbook for the Sixteen Personality Factor Questionnaire (16PF). Champaign, Illinois: Institute for Personality and Ability Testing.

_____. 1972. Manual for the 16PF. Champaign, Illinois: Institute for Personality and Ability Testing.

_____ and K. E. Nichols. 1972. "An Improved Definition from Ten Researches, of Second Order Personality Factors in Q-Data (with

Cross-Cultural Checks)," <u>Journal of Social Psychology</u>. 86:187-203.

Cattell, Raymond B. and G. F. Stice. 1954. "Four Formulae for Selecting Leaders on the Basis of Personality," <u>Human Relations</u>. 7:493-507.

_____, D. F. Tatro, and E. Komlos. 1964. "The Diagnosis and Inferred Structure of Paranoid and Non-paranoid Schizophrenia from the 16PF Profile (I. Installment)," <u>Indian Psychological Review</u>. I:52-61.

_____, D. F. Tatro, and E. Komlos. 1965. "The Diagnosis and Inferred Structure of Paranoid and Non-paranoid Schizophrenia from the 16PF Profile (II. Concluding Installment)," <u>Indian Psychological Review</u>. I:108-115.

Constantine, Joan and Larry Constantine. 1974. "Jealosy - the Marriage Killer," <u>Penthouse Forum</u>. March:59-60.

Daly, Liam. 1975. "Family Violence: A Psychiatric Perspective," Journal of the Irish Medical Association. Dublin, Ireland. 68(18):450-453.

Delhees, K. H. and R. B. Cattell. 1970. "Obtaining 16PF Scores from the MMPI, and MMPI Scores from the 16PF," <u>Journal of Projective Techniques and Personality Assessment</u>. 34:251-255.

Durbin, Karen. 1974. "Wife-beating," <u>Ladies' Home Journal</u>. June: 62:64-65, 67, 72.

English, Horace B. and Ava C. English. 1970. _A Comprehensive Dictionary of Psychological and Psychoanalytical Terms_. New York: David McKay Company, Inc.

Eysenck, H. J. 1953. _The Scientific Study of Personality_. London, England: Tavistock Publications.

Eysenck, J. J. 1961. "Classification and the Problem of Diagnosis," _Handbook of Abnormal Psychology_. H. J. Eysenck, ed. New York: Basic Books, 1-31.

Federal Bureau of Investigation. 1974. _Uniform Crime Reports for the United States_. Washington, D.C.: U.S. Government Printing Office, 223.

Fitts, William H. 1965. _Manual, Tennessee Self Concept Scale_. Nashville: Tennessee Department of Mental Health.

_____. 1973. _Monograph Series on the Self Concept_. Nashville: Counselor Recordings and Tests.

Francke, Linda Bird. 1976. "Battered Wives," _Newsweek_. 2 February: 47-48.

Freud, Anna. 1974. _The Ego and the Mechanisms of Defense_. (1936) New York: International Universities Press, Inc.

Freud, Sigmund. 1974. _The Ego and the Id_. (1923). London: Hogarth.

Gayford, J. J. 1975. "Wife Battering, A Preliminary Survey of 100 Cases," <u>British Medical Journal</u>. January 1: 194-197.

_____. 1975. "Battered Wives," <u>Medicine, Science and the Law</u>. 15(4):237-245.

Gelles, Richard J. 1972. <u>The Violent Home</u>. Beverly Hills, California: Sage Publications.

_____. 1976. "Abused Wives: Why Do They Stay?", in Press.

_____. 1975. "Violence and Pregnancy: A Note on the Extent of the Problem and Needed Services," <u>The Family Coordinator</u>. 24(1): 81-96.

Gibbens, T.C.N. 1975. "Violence in the Family," <u>Medico-legal Journal</u>. 43(3):76-88.

Gividen, G. M. 1958. "Stress in Airborne Training as Related to the Self-concept, Motivation and Biographical Factors," Unpublished masters' thesis. Vanderbilt University.

Goode, William J. 1971. "Force and Violence in the Family," <u>Journal of Marriage and the Family</u>. November: 624-636.

Kelley, E. L. 1955. "Consistency of the Adult Personality," <u>American Psychologist</u>. 10: 659-681.

Kennedy, Wallace A. 1971. <u>Child Psychology</u>. Englewood Cliffs, New Jersey: Prentice-Hall, Inc.

Kerlinger, Fred N. 1973. Foundations of Behavioral Research. New York: Holt, Rinehart and Winston, Inc.

Krug, Samuel E. and Raymond B. Cattell. 1971. "A Test of the 'Trait-view' Theory of Distortion in Measurement of Personality by Questionnaire," Educational and Psychological Measurement, in Press.

_____ and J. E. Laughlin. 1976. "Second-order Factors Among Normal and Pathological Primary Personality Traits," Journal of Consulting and Clinical Psychology, in Press.

Langley, Roger and Richard C. Levy. 1977. Wife Beating: The Silent Crisis. New York: E. P. Dutton.

Lefeber, James. 1964. "The Delinquent's Self-perception." Unpublished Doctoral dissertation, Los Angeles: University of Southern California.

Levin, May Jackson. 1975. "The Wife Beaters," McCalls. June: 37.

Lystad, Mary Hanemann. 1975. "Violence at Home," American Journal of Orthopsychiatry. 45(3):328-345.

Marsden, Dennis and David Owens. 1975. "The Jekyll and Hyde Marriages," New Society. 32(657):333-335.

Martin, Del. 1976. Battered Wives. San Francisco: Glide Publications.

Maslow, Abraham H. 1971. The Further Reaches of Human Nature. New York: Viking Press.

Meredith, Gerald M. 1968. "Stereotype Desirability Profiles for the 16PF Questionnaire," Psychological Reports. 23(3, Pt 2):1173-1174.

Minium, Edward W. 1970. Statistical Reasoning in Psychology and Education. New York: John Wiley and Sons, Inc.

Mischel, Walter. 1969. "Continuity and Change in Personality," American Psychologist. 24:1012-1018.

Moore, Jean G. 1975. "The Yo-Yo Syndrome: A Matter for Interdisciplinary Concern," Medicine, Science and the Law. 15(4):234-236.

MS. 1976. August: 51-52, 54, 94, 95-98.

Newman, Jill. 1976. "How Battered Wives are Fighting Back," Los Angeles Times, Parade Magazine Section, April: 26.

Newsweek. 1973. "Battered Wives," 9 July: 29.

Nichols, Beverly B. 1975. "The Abused Wife Problem," Social Casework. 57(1):27-32.

Pagelow, Mildred D. 1976. "Preliminary Report on Battered Women," Sociological study. (Mimeographed.)

Piety, K. R. 1958. "The Role of Defense in Reporting on the Self Concept." Unpublished Doctoral dissertation, Vanderbilt University.

Pizzey, Erin. 1974. *Scream Quietly or the Neighbors Will Hear*. Baltimore, Maryland: Penguin Books, Inc.

_____. 1974. "Violence Begins at Home," *The London Spectator*. 23 November.

Reif, Adelbert. 1975. "Eric Fromm on Human Aggression," *Psychology Today*. April: 22-23.

Saul, Leon J. 1972. "Personal and Social Psychopathology and the Primary Prevention of Violence," *American Journal of Psychiatry*. 12:128-131.

Scott, P. D. 1974. "Battered Wives," *British Journal of Psychiatry*. 125:433-441.

Schmidt, H. O. and C. P. Fonda. 1956. "The Reliability of Psychiatric Diagnosis: A New Look," *Journal of Social Psychology*. 52: 262-267.

Schuyler, Marcella. 1976. "Battered Wives: An Emerging Social Problem," *Social Work*. 21(6): 488-491.

Snell, John E., Richard J. Rosenwald, and Ames Robey. 1964. "The Wifebeater's Wife," *Archives of General Psychiatry*. 11:107-112.

Stark, Rodney and James McEvoy III. 1970. "Middle Class Violence," *Psychology Today*. November: 30-32.

Steinmetz, Suzanne K. and Murray Straus, ed. 1975. *Violence in the Family*. New York: Dodd, Mean and Co.

Straus, Murray A. 1975. "Leveling, Civility and Violence in the Family," Journal of Marriage and the Family. February: 13-29.

Sullivan, H. S. 1953. The Interpersonal Theory of Psychiatry. New York: Norton Press.

Tomalin, Caroline. 1974. "Refuge for Battered Women," Health and Social Service Journal. 84(4388):1169.

Truninger, Elizabeth. 1971. "Marital Violence: The Legal Solutions," Hastings Law Journal. 23(1):262.

Turner, Ralph H. 1970. Family Interaction. New York: John Wiley and Sons, Inc.

Warrior, Betsy. 1975. "Battered Lives," Houseworker's Handbook. (Mimeographed.)

_____. 1976. "Sexual Inequality, Cultural Norms, and Wife Beating." Sociological study. (Mimeographed.)

_____. 1976. "Working on Wife Abuse." Listing. (Mimeographed.)

Weitzman, Lenore. 1974. "Legal Regulation of Marriage: Tradition and Change," California Law Review. 62(4):1170-1187.

Wells, W. S. and L. F. Bueno. 1957. "A Self-concept Measure of Male and Female Alcoholics." Unpublished manuscript.

Whitaker, Carl A. 1975. "Psychotherapy of the Absurd With a Special Emphasis on the Psychotherapy of Aggression," Family Process. 14(1):1-16.

Whitehurst, Robert N. 1971. "Violence Potential in Extramarital Sexual Responses," *Journal of Marriage and the Family*. November: 683-691.

_____. 1971. "Violently Jealous Husbands," *Sexual Behavior*. July: 41.

Winter, William D. and Antonio J. Ferreira, eds. 1969. *Research and Family Interaction Readings and Commentary*. Palo Alto, California: Science and Behavior Books, Inc.

Wolfgang, Marvin E. 1958. *Patterns of Criminal Homicide*. Philadelphia: University of Pennsylvania Press.

Wolman, Benjamin B. 1965. *Handbook of Clinical Psychology*. New York: McGraw-Hill Inc.

_____. 1973. *Dictionary of Behavioral Science*. New York: Van Nostrand Reinhold Company.

APPENDIX

APPENDIX A

Descriptions of Subjects

Table 7

Race of Subjects

Racial Group	Wife Groups	
	Battered (N=30)	Non-Battered (N=30)
Caucasian	26	28
Black	1	1
Mexican-American	2	1
Oriental	1	0

Table 8

Religion of Subjects

Religious Group	Wife Groups	
	Battered (N=30)	Non-Battered (N=30)
Catholic	4	5
Protestant	18	17
Jewish	2	3
Other	1	1
None	5	4

Table 9

Educational Level of Subjects

Level Completed	Wife Groups	
	Battered (N=30)	Non-Battered (N=30)
Less than 8th grade	0	0
9 - 12 grade	1	2
High school graduate	27	24
Some college	1	2
College graduate or higher	1	2

Table 10

Marital Status of Subjects

Marital Status	Wife Groups	
	Battered (N=30)	Non-Battered (N=30)
Married	22	21
Divorced	2	4
Separated	3	2
Widow	1	2
Living together, unmarried	2	1

Table 11

Length of Time Married of Subjects

Time Length	Wife Groups	
	Battered (N=30)	Non-Battered (N=30)
One week to 3 years	3	1
4 to 8 years	9	4
9 to 13 years	10	9
14 to 18 years	7	12
Over 18 years	1	4
Mean Length	10.2	13.1

Table 12

Number of Children of Subjects

Number of Children	Wife Groups	
	Battered (N=30)	Non-Battered (N=30)
0	5	3
1	2	4
2	10	11
3	8	5
4	3	2
5	1	2
Over 5	1	3
Mean Number	2.7	2.4

Table 13

Occupations of Husbands of Subjects

Husband's Occupational Group	Wife Groups	
	Battered (N=30)	Non-Battered (N=30)
Professional/ technical	2	1
Managerial/ proprietor	3	5
Sales and clerical	7	6
Craftsman/foreman	3	4
Military (Enl. & Off.)	8	7
Operators/cook/ bartender	1	2
Laborer/ truck driver	3	3
Unemployed	3	2

Table 14

Occupation of Subjects

Subject's Occupational Group	Wife Groups	
	Battered (N=30)	Non-Battered (N=30)
Professional/ technical	0	1
Managerial/ Proprietress	1	1
Medical - nurse, aide, technician	2	3
Education - teacher, aide	1	2
Secretarial/ clerical	5	10
Waitress	6	4
Domestic/laborer	3	2
Unemployed/ housewife	12	7

Table 15

Total Family Income of Subjects

Amount of Income (Yearly)	Wife Groups	
	Battered (N=30)	Non-Battered (N=30)
Under $4,999	0	0
$5,000 - $6,999	3	1
$7,000 - $9,999	11	12
$10,000 - $14,999	10	9
$15,000 - $19,999	4	6
$20,000 or higher	2	2
Mean Income	$11,900	$15,000

Table 16

Age of Subjects

Age in Years	Wife Groups	
	Battered (N=30)	Non-Battered (N=30)
16 - 25	5	3
26 - 35	9	7
36 - 45	11	8
46 - 55	3	7
56 - 65	2	5
Over 65	0	0
Mean Age	33.6	37.9

APPENDIX B

Summary of Means and Standard Deviations
for the 16PF and TSCS Scores

Table 17

Summary of the Mean Sixteen Personality
Factor Scores for the Battered (N=30)
and Non-Battered Wife Groups (N=30)

Factor	Battered Mean	SD	Non-Battered Mean	SD
A	5.17	2.20	6.10	1.16
B	6.33	1.81	6.53	1.53
C	4.33	1.75	6.57	1.50
E	5.57	2.25	5.93	2.00
F	5.43	2.73	5.67	2.23
G	6.17	2.31	5.80	1.92
H	5.93	2.53	7.07	2.49
I	5.77	1.46	5.20	1.56
L	6.23	1.83	5.57	1.59
M	4.70	2.05	4.80	1.67
N	6.10	1.11	5.73	1.74
O	6.80	2.07	4.00	1.55
Q_1	6.40	2.36	5.40	1.65
Q_2	5.60	2.61	5.40	2.11
Q_3	4.40	2.51	6.73	1.86
Q_4	7.33	1.18	5.13	1.61
Extraversion	5.75	2.49	6.30	2.11
Anxiety	6.94	1.43	4.36	1.18
Tough Poise	6.01	1.73	6.62	1.58
Independence	5.41	2.13	5.63	1.67
Neuroticism	6.61	1.86	4.57	1.48
Leadership	5.28	2.11	7.08	1.50
Creativity	6.03	2.26	5.62	1.93

Table 18

Summary of the Mean Tennessee Self Concept
Scale Scores for the Battered (N=30)
and Non-Battered Wife Groups (N=30)

Factor	Battered Mean	SD	Non-Battered Mean	SD
Self-criticism	50.43	12.28	51.33	8.81
Self-esteem	40.07	15.34	59.33	11.52
Row 1 Identity	36.03	18.58	56.73	10.89
Row 2 Self-satisfaction	43.87	14.15	60.23	11.25
Row 3 Behavior	40.67	13.93	56.70	11.19
Col A Physical self	32.87	17.35	48.70	14.08
Col B Moral-ethical	44.43	16.60	59.80	8.42
Col C Personal self	43.83	14.44	61.30	11.62
Col D Family self	38.37	17.14	58.63	10.89
Col E Social self	44.47	15.12	58.43	9.28
Defensive Positive	46.77	10.74	56.40	7.93
General Maladjustment	63.63	15.02	43.53	12.00
Psychosis	61.10	14.82	49.00	10.75
Personality Disorder	57.27	14.35	44.27	7.26
Neurosis	62.17	14.73	44.87	11.10
Personality Integration	40.23	12.59	48.67	9.25
Total Conflict	53.30	12.24	47.63	11.05
Total Variability	51.60	10.10	42.20	8.86
D_5	49.77	11.05	54.93	12.46
D_4	52.67	12.69	48.30	11.81
D_3	51.30	10.98	44.50	12.64
D_2	47.17	10.29	41.70	8.18
D_1	45.80	13.42	55.80	10.24

APPENDIX C

The Questionnaires

Sixteen Personality Factor Questionnaire (16PF)

The questionnaire and all related materials have been copyrighted, and may be obtained from the Institute for Personality and Ability Testing, 1602 Coronado Drive, Champaign, Illinois, 61820, by persons substantiating training and supervised experience in the clinical use of psychological instruments.

Tennessee Self Concept Scale (TSCS)

The questionnaire, manual, and Clinical and Research Form answer sheet have been copyrighted by William H. Fitts, and may be obtained from Counselor Recordings and Tests, Box 6184 - Acklen Station, Nashville, Tennessee, 37212, by persons who can substantiate training and supervised experience in the clinical use of psychological tests.

THE EVANS LIBRARY
FULTON-MONTGOMERY COMMUNITY COLLEGE
2805 STATE HIGHWAY 67
JOHNSTOWN, NEW YORK 12095-3790